Giraffes and Zebras

Michael and Jane Pelusey

Marshall Cavendish
Benchmark
New York

Marshall Cavendish Benchmark
99 White Plains Road
Tarrytown, NY 10591
www.marshallcavendish.us

First published in 2008 by
MACMILLAN EDUCATION AUSTRALIA PTY LTD
15–19 Claremont Street, South Yarra 3141

Visit our Web site at www.macmillan.com.au or go directly to www.macmillanlibrary.com.au

Associated companies and representatives throughout the world.

Library of Congress Cataloging-in-Publication Data

Pelusey, Michael.
    Giraffes and zebras / by Michael and Jane Pelusey.
    p. cm. — (Zoo animals)
    Includes index.
    ISBN 978-0-7614-3149-7
    1. Giraffe—Juvenile literature. 2. Zebras—Juvenile literature.
    3. Zoo animals—Juvenile literature. I. Title.
    SF408.6.G57P45 2008
    636.9638—dc22

                                                            2008001655

Edited by Margaret Maher
Text and cover design by Christine Deering
Page layout by Christine Deering
Illustrations by Gaston Vanzet

Printed in the United States

Acknowledgments
Michael and Jane Pelusey would like to thank Perth Zoo, Melbourne Zoo, Werribee Wildlife Zoo, and Taronga Zoo for their assistance with this project.

Cover photograph: Giraffes feeding at a wildlife zoo, courtesy of Pelusey Photography.

All photographs © Pelusey Photography except for © Dragoneye/Dreamstime.com, **29**; © Lord.max/ Dreamstime.com, **28**; Global Gypsies, **10**, **11**; Werribee Wildlife Zoo, **19**, **22** (right).

Contents

Glossary words

When a word is printed in **bold**, you can look up its meaning in the Glossary on page 31.

Zoos

Zoos are places where animals that are usually **wild** are kept in **enclosures**. Some zoos have a lot of space for animals to move about. They are called wildlife zoos.

Large animals, such as giraffes, have plenty of space in a wildlife zoo.

Zoo Animals

Zoos keep all kinds of animals. People go to zoos to learn about animals. Some animals may become **extinct** if left to live in the wild.

People learn about animals that come from other countries at a zoo.

Giraffes and Zebras

Giraffes are the world's tallest animals. They have long legs and very long necks. Each giraffe has a different pattern of brown patches on its skin.

long neck

brown patches on skin

long legs

Giraffes' long necks help them reach food in high places.

Zebras are related to horses. They live in **herds**. Each zebra has a different pattern of black and white stripes.

black and white stripes

Living in herds helps protect zebras from animals that might hunt them.

In the Wild

In the wild, zebras are found in the southern half of Africa. Giraffes are found in a larger area of Africa.

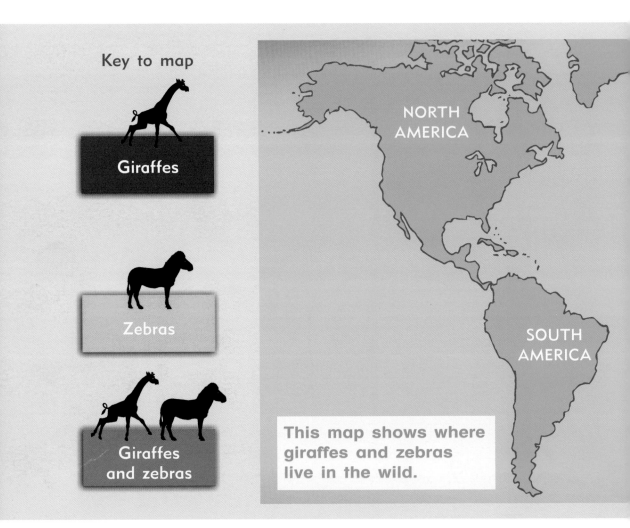

Key to map

Giraffes

Zebras

Giraffes and zebras

NORTH AMERICA

SOUTH AMERICA

This map shows where giraffes and zebras live in the wild.

Giraffes and zebras are often found together on the **savannas** of Africa. Giraffes **graze** on leaves from tall trees. Zebras eat grass from the ground.

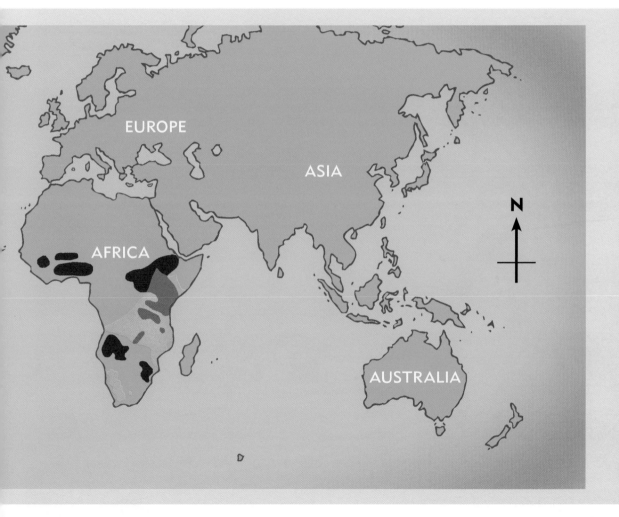

Threats to Survival

The biggest threat to the survival of giraffes and zebras is the clearing of land for farms.

Large areas of savanna have been cleared for farms and villages.

Poachers sometimes hunt giraffes for their fur, meat, and tails. Some kinds of zebras are **endangered**.

Some endangered zebras are kept in zoos.

A giraffe's fur is valuable to poachers.

Zoo Homes

In zoos, giraffes and zebras live in enclosures.
These enclosures are often built so they are like
the giraffes' and zebras' homes in the wild.

trees for shade

leaves in the trees
for giraffes to eat

sand for zebras to roll in

water to drink

hay on the ground for
zebras to eat

This enclosure has trees and water for the giraffes and zebras.

Giraffes and zebras have space to roam at a wildlife zoo.

Many wildlife enclosures are similar to the giraffes' home in the wild.

13

Zoo Food

Giraffes and zebras need to eat different types of food to stay healthy.

A giraffe's zoo food

lucerne hay

pellets made from a mixture of barley, oats, and **molasses**

acacia leaves

Give the giraffes daily treats of apples, bananas, and weeping willow leaves.

A zebra's zoo food

11 pounds (5 kg) lucerne hay

grass

Giraffes eat lucerne hay each day.

Feeding

The zebras' food is placed on the ground. The giraffes' food is placed high in a tree where only they can reach it.

Zebras eat hay left for them on the ground.

Zoo Health

Zookeepers look after the giraffes and zebras so the animals stay healthy. The keepers stand on a high platform to check the giraffes for any health problems.

The keepers look at the skin, eyes, and mouth of a giraffe during a health check.

Zookeepers count the zebras when they feed them. The zookeepers also check that the zebras are healthy and not injured.

The keepers stay inside the van when they check on the zebras.

Baby Giraffes and Zebras

Giraffes have one baby at a time. It takes fourteen months for a **calf** to grow inside its mother. Giraffe calves can walk one hour after they are born.

A baby giraffe stays close to its mother.

Zebras have one **foal** at a time. It takes fourteen months for a baby zebra to grow inside its mother.

A zebra is born with brown stripes that turn black as the zebra grows up.

How Zoos Are Saving Giraffes and Zebras

Zoos help save giraffes and zebras. The Rothschild giraffe and Grevy's zebra, a large type of zebra, are both endangered in the wild. Zoos **breed** these animals to save them from becoming extinct.

Rothschild giraffes have a bump, like a horn, in the middle of their foreheads.

Zoos also run special tours such as the Tall Order Giraffe Encounter. This raises money for giraffe breeding programs. Visitors get a close look at giraffes from a high platform.

The Tall Order Giraffe Encounter allows visitors to get close to giraffes.

Zoos around the world work together. Giraffes are often moved from one zoo to another for breeding.

This giraffe will be moved to another zoo for breeding.

Moving a giraffe is difficult because it is so tall. A special box is made to hold the giraffe. The giraffe is then taken by truck to its new home.

A giraffe travels in a specially made box on the back of a truck.

The giraffe joins other giraffes at a new zoo.

Meet Debbie, a Giraffe Keeper

Debbie gives a branch of leaves to a giraffe.

Question   How did you become a zookeeper?

Answer   I have always loved animals. I studied to be a zookeeper.

Question   How long have you been a keeper?

Answer   I have been a zookeeper for six years.

Debbie also looks after the rhinoceroses.

Question What animals have you worked with?

Answer I have worked mainly with African animals, such as giraffes and rhinoceroses.

Question What do you like about your job?

Answer Each animal has a different personality. It is interesting and exciting.

A Day in the Life of a Zookeeper

Zookeepers have certain jobs to do each day.
At a wildlife zoo, zookeepers work with giraffes, zebras,
and other animals.

8:00 a.m.

Count the zebra herd to make sure they are all there.

9:00 a.m.

Give the giraffes a treat of pellets.

10:00 a.m.

Feed the zebras some hay.

4:00 p.m.

Place a branch with leaves in the enclosure for the giraffes to eat.

Zoos Around the World

There are many zoos around the world. The Berlin Zoo is located in Berlin, in Germany. It keeps more than 1,500 kinds of animal, including giraffes and zebras.

This baby zebra was born at the Berlin Zoo.

Some of the animals at the Berlin Zoo are kept in modern enclosures. Other animals are kept in enclosures that were built many years ago.

The famous giraffe enclosure is more than 130 years old.

The Importance of Zoos

Zoos do very important work. They:

- help people learn about animals
- save endangered animals and animals that are treated badly

Rothschild giraffes are increasing in numbers with the help of zoos.

Glossary

acacia   a type of tree, also known as wattle

breed   keep animals so that they can produce babies

calf   a baby giraffe

enclosures   the fenced areas where animals are kept in zoos

endangered   at a high risk of becoming extinct

extinct   no longer living on Earth

foal   a baby zebra

graze   eat throughout the day

herds   a large group of animals

molasses   a sugary liquid made from sugarcane

pellets   small balls of dried food

poachers   people who hunt animals illegally

savannas   grasslands with scattered trees

wild   living in its natural environment and not taken care of by humans

Index